新年好 We Love 新年好
CHINESE NEW YEAR

Saviour Pirotta

WAYLAND

© copyright Wayland 2006

Editor: Kirsty Hamilton
Senior Design Manager: Rosamund Saunders
Designer: Elaine Wilkinson

Published in Great Britain in 2006 by Wayland,
an imprint of Hachette Children's Books

British Library Cataloguing in Publication Data
Pirotta, Saviour
We love Chinese New Year
1.Chinese New Year – Juvenile literature
I.Title
394.2'614'0951

ISBN 10: 0 7502 4589 1
ISBN 13: 978 0 7502 4589 0

Printed in China

Wayland
An imprint of Hachette Children's Books
338 Euston Road, London NW1 3BH

The publishers would like to thank the following for
allowing us to reproduce their pictures in this book:

Alamy: 4, IPS; 6, A.Parada; 7, Oote Boe; 8, Beaconstox; 9,
Jon Bower; 13, Photowood Inc; Kevin Foy, 16; 21, Ryan
Ghail / Getty: 10, Don Smetzer, Stone; cover, 20, Billy
Hustace, Stone / Corbis: 12, 17, 23, Keren Su; 14, Dave G.
Houser; 15, Phil Schermeister; title page, 18, 19, Kevin
Fleming; Wayland Picture Library: 5, 11.

Contents 新年好

新
年
好

Happy New Year

Gung Hei Fat Choi! That means Happy New Year in Chinese.

新年好

The plum blossom is a **symbol** of hope for the new year.

4

The Chinese New Year starts at the
end of winter, in late January or early
February. That's when new plants begin
to appear in the garden and leaves are
getting ready to open on the trees.

Farmers all
over China
plough the
earth, ready
to **sow** their
new crops.

Get ready for the party

新年好

New Year is the perfect time for a haircut.

Chinese New Year celebrations can last up to fifteen days. But there's a lot to do before people can start enjoying themselves.

Houses are cleaned from top to bottom. People decorate their homes with fruit and beautiful flowers. They also have their hair cut and buy new clothes.

Oranges are bought for good luck. They make you rich!

DID YOU KNOW?

Everyone prays to the Kitchen God. He will tell the Jade Emperor how good the family have been!

7

Good luck everyone!

People write short poems on red **banners** trimmed with gold. They hang the banners around the house to bring blessings and good luck.

Shops sell banners with poems and messages of good wishes for the New Year.

新年好

8

Some families hang pictures of the **door gods** outside the front door. They believe the gods will guard the house against ghosts and bad luck.

新年好

Sometimes **incense** is burnt, to remember relatives that have died.

9

Goodbye old year

The celebrations start on New Year's Eve. All over the world, Chinese people turn on bright lights. Families get together and eat a special dinner.

It's time for a delicious feast.

新年好

Dumplings have tasty savoury fillings.

In the north of China, people enjoy **dumplings**. In the south they eat a delicious rice pudding.

Where's the monster?

All that banging should give the monster a headache!

There's an old story in China about a horrible monster called Nian. He liked eating people up. To scare Nian away, the people started banging drums and **gongs** and burning **bamboo** sticks.

Chinese people make a lot of noise
on New Year's Eve, to keep the
monster away.

It's fun
to watch
fireworks
on New
Year's Eve.

13

Lucky packets

新年好

On New Year's Day, people put on their new clothes. They visit their friends and relatives to wish them a Happy New Year. Families offer visitors delicious nibbles that bring good luck.

This tangerine tree has been decorated with lucky red bows.

The envelopes are coloured red for good luck.

The grown-ups give children red envelopes with lucky symbols on them. Inside there is money. It's the perfect New Year gift.

Don't do it!

People are very careful on New Year's Day. No one sweeps the floor, in case they brush away all the good luck. Nobody uses scissors, in case they snip all the good luck away.

Nobody argues or scowls on New Year's Day.

Everyone is very careful not to break anything. That would bring bad luck.

People put on operas to celebrate the New Year. Each area has its own style and story.

DID YOU KNOW?

On New Year's Day people don't wash their hair, in case they flush their good luck down the plughole!

Dance, dragon, dance

The longer the dragon, the more luck it will bring.

During the New Year festival, many people come out to watch the famous **dragon** dance.

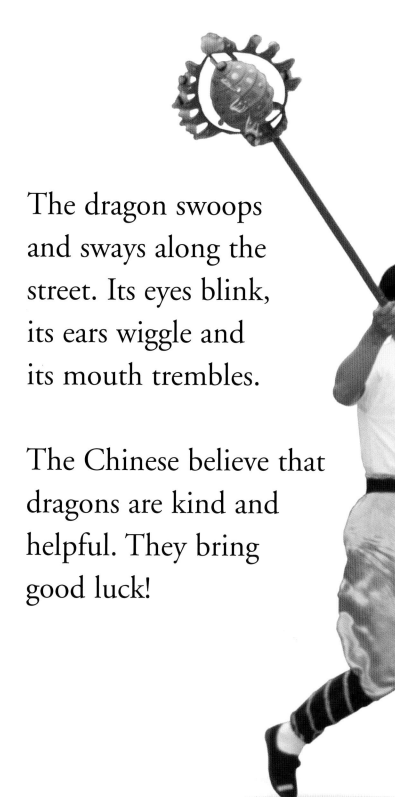

The dragon swoops and sways along the street. Its eyes blink, its ears wiggle and its mouth trembles.

The Chinese believe that dragons are kind and helpful. They bring good luck!

The dragon follows a leader, who carries a **lantern** on a long stick.

Light your lantern

新年許

These children have dressed up in red for the lantern parade.

On the last day of the New Year celebrations, people have a lantern festival. Paper lanterns are hung up everywhere. Children take part in a parade, carrying lanterns along the streets.

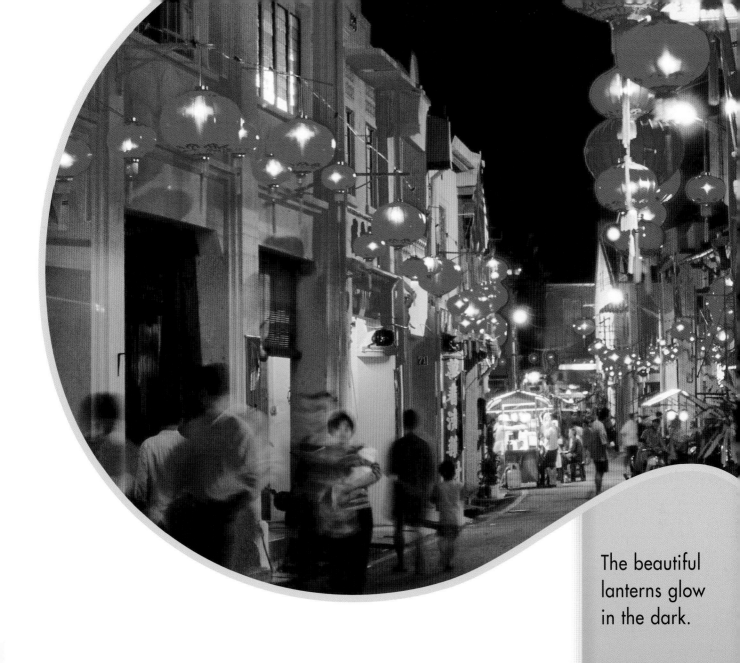

The beautiful lanterns glow in the dark.

What a wonderful ending to the New Year celebrations. Let's do it all again next year.

21

The Chinese calendar

The years in the Chinese calendar are all named after animals. There are twelve animals in all. Find your birthday on our calendar and see what Chinese year you were born in.

Rabbit	1987	1999
Dragon	1988	2000
Snake	1989	2001
Horse	1990	2002
Ram	1991	2003
Monkey	1992	2004
Rooster	1993	2005
Dog	1994	2006
Boar	1995	2007
Rat	1996	2008
Ox	1997	2009
Tiger	1998	2010

Gung Hei Fat Choi!

Index and glossary

bamboo a giant woody grass that grows in China

banner a large sign with writing, usually on cloth

door gods two fierce warriors, thought to frighten away evil spirits

dragon a mythical fire-breathing monster

dumplings boiled parcels of food, made from suet, flour and water

gong a metal disk that makes a note when hit

plough to loosen soil to get rid of weeds or prepare for planting

incense tree gum or spice that makes a sweet smell when burnt

lantern a lamp with a case around it to protect the flame

sow to plant seeds in the earth

symbol something that represents something else